Bettendorf Public Library
Information Center
www.bettendorflibrary.com

WIT

D1462794

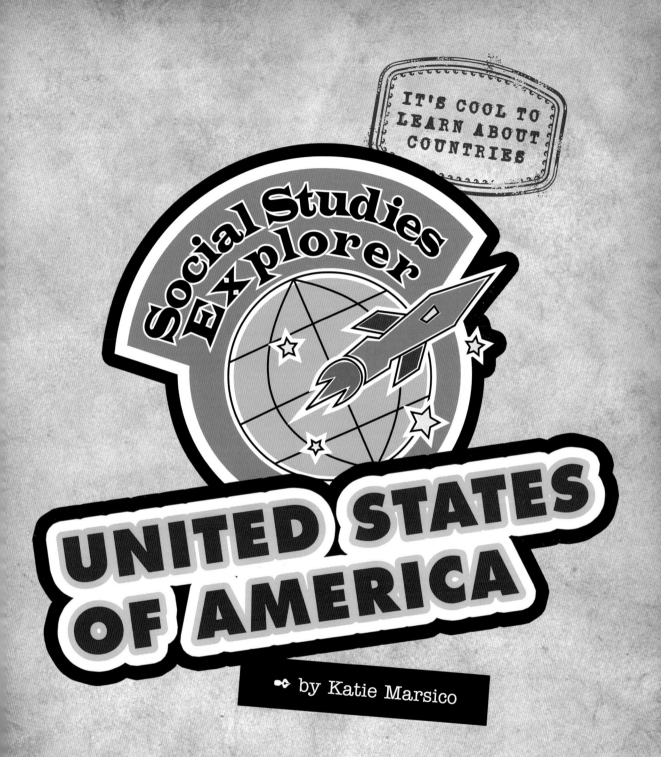

IT'S COOL TO LEARN ABOUT COUNTRIES

Social Studies Explorer

# UNITED STATES OF AMERICA

by Katie Marsico

CHERRY LAKE PUBLISHING • ANN ARBOR, MICHIGAN

Published in the United States of America
by Cherry Lake Publishing
Ann Arbor, Michigan
www.cherrylakepublishing.com

Content Adviser: Adrea Lawrence, PhD, Assistant Professor, School of Education, Teaching & Health, American University, Washington, DC

Book design: The Design Lab

Photo credits: Cover, ©gary718/Shutterstock, Inc.; cover and pages 3, 20 top, 23 bottom, 27 top, 29 top, 37 top, 39, and 48 top, ©iStockphoto.com/leezsnow; cover and pages 7 bottom, 17, 23 top, 24, 27 bottom, 29 bottom, 37 bottom, 40 bottom, 48 bottom, ©iStockphoto.com/bluestocking; page 4, ©Amy Nichole Harris/Shutterstock, Inc.; page 5, ©Mariusz S. Jurgielewicz/Shutterstock, Inc.; page 7 top, ©Ramunas Bruzas/Shutterstock, Inc.; page 8, ©iofoto/Shutterstock, Inc.; page 9, ©TOSP Photo/Shutterstock, Inc.; page 11, ©Sam Chadwick/Shutterstock, Inc.; page 12, ©A Cotton Photo/Shutterstock, Inc.; page 13, ©iStockphoto.com/kledge; page 14, ©iStockphoto.com/akurtz; page 16, ©Andrew Gentry/Shutterstock, Inc.; page 18, ©Thomas Weissenfels/Shutterstock, Inc.; page 19, ©Rrodrickbeiler/Dreamstime.com; page 21, ©Christopher Futcher/Shutterstock, Inc.; page 22 top left, ©Erwin Wodicka/Shutterstock, Inc.; page 22 top right, ©Mikhail Tchkheidze/Shutterstock, Inc.; page 22 bottom, ©Joao Virissimo/Shutterstock, Inc.; page 25, ©kristian sekulic/Shutterstock, Inc.; page 26, ©Yanfei Sun/Shutterstock, Inc.; page 28, ©Laurin Rinder/Shutterstock, Inc.; page 30, ©Christoff/Shutterstock, Inc.; page 34, ©iStockphoto.com/sjlocke; page 35, ©Henryk Sadura/Shutterstock, Inc.; page 36, ©ClassicStock/Alamy; page 38, ©Michael Onisiforou/Shutterstock, Inc.; page 40 top, ©Stephen Mcsweeny/Shutterstock, Inc.; page 41, ©Joy Brown/Shutterstock, Inc.; page 42, ©Inga Nielsen/Shutterstock, Inc.; page 43, ©iStockphoto.com/tazytaz; page 45, ©Hannamariah/Shutterstock, Inc.

Copyright ©2011 by Cherry Lake Publishing
All rights reserved. No part of this book may be reproduced or utilized in
any form or by any means without written permission from the publisher.

Library of Congress Cataloging-in-Publication Data
Marsico, Katie, 1980-
  It's cool to learn about countries: United States/by Katie Marsico.
      p. cm.—(Social studies explorer)
  Includes bibliographical references and index.
  ISBN-13: 978-1-60279-825-0 (lib. bdg.)
  ISBN-10: 1-60279-825-7 (lib. bdg.)
  1. United States—Juvenile literature. I. Title. II. Title: United States. III. Series.
  E156.M36 2011
  973—dc22                                          2009048562

Cherry Lake Publishing would like to acknowledge the work of The Partnership for
21st Century Skills. Please visit www.21stcenturyskills.org for more information.

Printed in the United States of America
Corporate Graphics Inc.
July 2010
CLFA07

J 973
MA

# TABLE OF CONTENTS

# CHAPTER ONE

# WELCOME TO THE UNITED STATES!

➤ The Statue of Liberty is a symbol of the United States. It was a gift from the people of France.

Would you like to explore the United States? The United States is a **diverse** nation. There are always plenty of new things to learn about and many interesting places to visit.

The United States is the world's third-largest country, after Russia and Canada. The people who live and work there represent many different cultures. This is why the United States is a land filled with so many unique foods, celebrations, and traditions.

As you explore, you might want to take in the towering redwood trees along California's Pacific Coast. Or you could stop by Walt Disney World Resort in Orlando, Florida, and hang with Mickey Mouse. Be sure to pay attention to all the sights, sounds, and tastes you'll experience along the way. Are you ready to start exploring the United States?

California's Pacific coastline offers many beautiful views of the ocean.

CANADA

UNITED STATES

Atlantic
Ocean

Pacific
Ocean

MEXICO

The United States shares borders with Canada and Mexico.

Look at a map of the world. Where is the United States located? This nation is part of the North American continent. The United States is bordered by Canada to the north. Mexico and the Gulf of Mexico are to the south. The Atlantic Ocean borders the country to the east, and the Pacific Ocean borders it to the west.

The country is made up of 50 states. Its capital is Washington, DC. The United States includes 3,794,100 square miles (9,826,675 square kilometers) of land and

water. When experts study the United States, they may divide the country in different ways. One way to consider the United States is to divide it into four main regions— the Northeast, the Midwest, the South, and the West.

The Northeast is famous for its diverse geography. For example, Maine is known for its rocky coastline. The Northeast also includes well-known mountain ranges such as New York's Adirondacks.

Puerto Rico, an island in the northeastern Caribbean Sea, is a commonwealth. As a commonwealth, Puerto Rico is allowed self-governing powers. Yet it is also considered a U.S. territory. Its people are recognized as U.S. citizens.

➥ Large barges carry goods up and down the Mississippi River.

Most of the Midwest features flat land. Farmers grow crops such as corn, soybeans, and wheat on the region's plains and prairies. The mighty Mississippi River helps supply water to Midwestern soil. The Mississippi is the nation's chief waterway.

As the Mississippi winds toward the Gulf of Mexico, it cuts across part of the South. This portion of the country also includes a wide range of geographic features, including mountains and **deltas**. When many people think of the South, however, they tend to picture humid

swamps, **bayous**, and marshes. These are commonly found in Florida and Louisiana.

The West is the nation's largest region. It is no surprise, then, that the West features all kinds of geography. The Rocky Mountains tower over Idaho, Montana, Wyoming, Utah, Colorado, New Mexico, and part of Washington. The Grand Canyon in Arizona plunges an astounding 5,249 feet (1,600 meters) at its deepest point. Lush green forests spread across states such as California, Oregon, and Washington. Certain regions of the West are also home to the Mojave, Sonoran, Great Basin, and Chihuahua deserts.

➾ The Grand Canyon is one of the most famous U.S. landmarks.

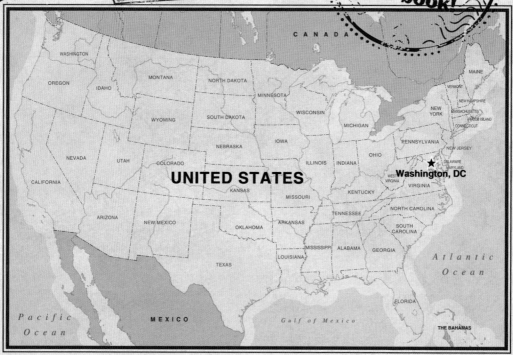

Check out this map of the United States. Use a separate piece of paper and trace the outline of the country. Draw a star to mark the location of Washington, DC. Use different colors of crayon or marker to divide the United States into the four geographic regions you have just read about. Draw some of the geographic features that were mentioned, too. Do you see how diverse U.S. geography is?

The United States' climate is just as diverse as its geography. Every region includes at least some areas with **temperate** weather. These sections of the country are usually known for their cold winters, warm springs, hot summers, and cooler autumns. The United States experiences extreme weather, too.

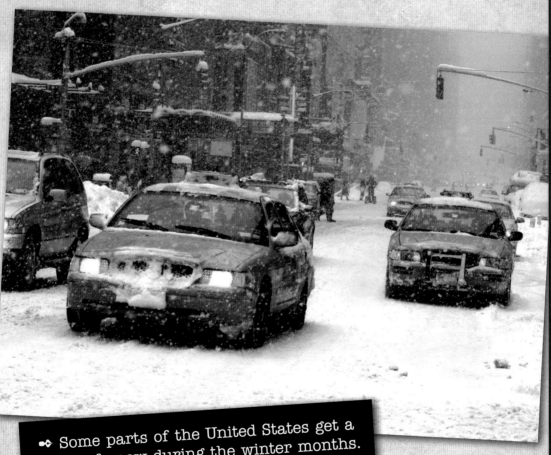

➥ Some parts of the United States get a lot of snow during the winter months.

Even the hottest and coldest parts of the country are home to a remarkable variety of life. Thousands of species of plants, animals, and other organisms live in the United States. Unfortunately, many of them are considered **endangered**. A few examples are gray wolves and bighorn sheep. Plants on the endangered list include black lace cactus and Texas wild rice. Keep an eye out for these species as you explore the United States.

The Florida manatee is an endangered animal that lives underwater.

CHAPTER TWO

UNITED STATES

# BUSINESS AND GOVERNMENT IN THE UNITED STATES

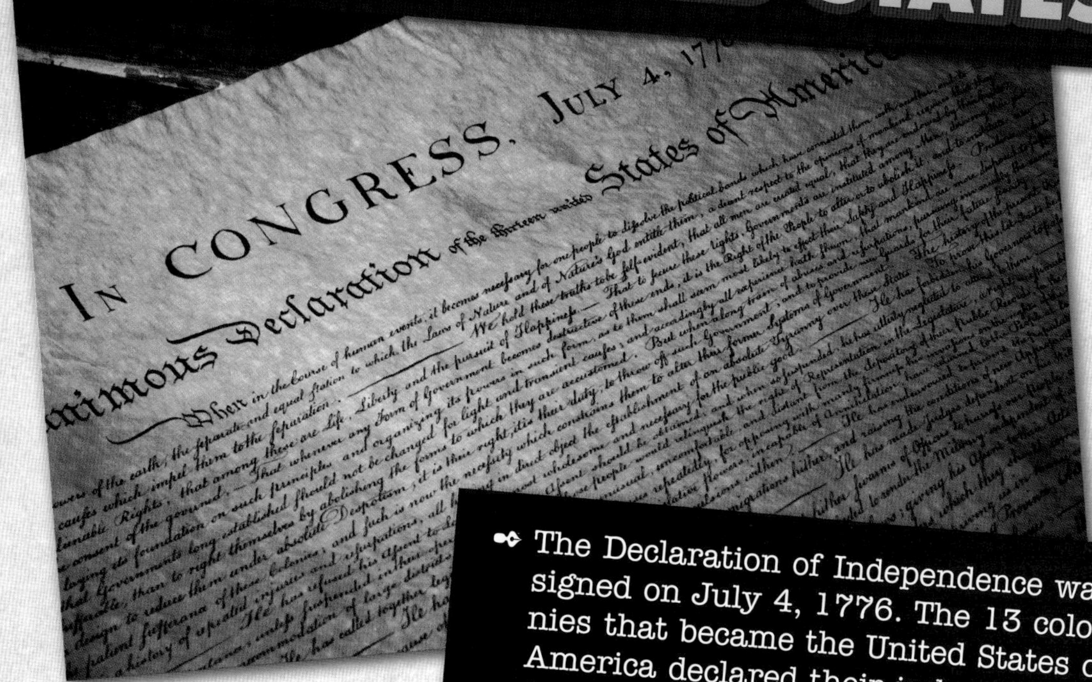

The Declaration of Independence was signed on July 4, 1776. The 13 colonies that became the United States of America declared their independence from Great Britain.

Compared to other nations that have existed for many centuries, the United States is a relatively young country. American colonists declared independence from Great Britain in 1776. War followed, and the Americans defeated the British in 1781 with help from France.

By 1783, the colonies had become the United States of America. The United States enjoyed a strong economy during the colonial period and as a young nation. The same is true today.

The United States attracts more than 1 million immigrants each year. They want better lives for themselves and their families. These men and women see the United States and its economy as an opportunity to achieve their dreams.

➽ U.S. citizens work at many different kinds of jobs.

In 2008, more than 154 million people were members of the U.S. workforce. Many are employed by companies that contributed to the $1.3 trillion in **exports** that were shipped to other countries that same year. The United States sells many different items to other nations. Some include soybeans, cars, chemicals, and medicines.

IMPORT EXPORT

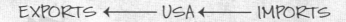

Do you want to know more about the U.S. economy? Take a look at its trading partners. Trading partners are the countries that **import** goods from a country or export goods to that country. Here is a graph showing the countries that are the United States' top import and export trading partners.

EXPORTS ⟵ USA ⟵ IMPORTS

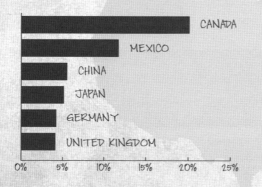

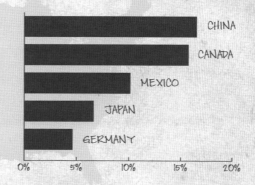

In the United States, services represent nearly 80 percent of the nation's business activity. The medical work that doctors perform is one type of service. Industry makes up 19 percent of business in the United States. People who have jobs in industry produce goods for sale. Major U.S. industries involve the production of oil, steel, and cars. Finally, agriculture forms slightly more than 1 percent of business activity. U.S. farmers help supply the world with fruits, vegetables, cotton, beef, pork, poultry, and dairy products.

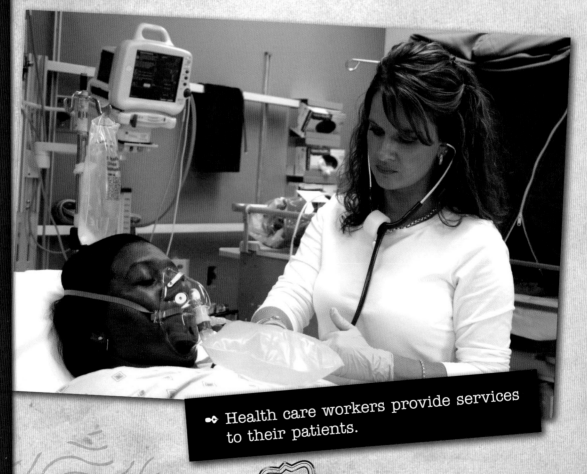

◆ Health care workers provide services to their patients.

In 2007, approximately 0.6 percent of American workers held jobs in farming, forestry, and fishing. Roughly 22 percent worked in areas such as manufacturing and transportation. Approximately 35 percent were employed in managerial, professional, and technical professions. Nearly 25 percent had sales and office jobs. Approximately 16 percent provided other services.

Use this information to create a bar graph that shows the different sections of the U.S. labor force. Ask a teacher or other adult for help if you need it.

STOP
Don't write in this book!

Experts usually describe the United States as having a mainly capitalist economy. This means that private individuals control most business activity. But the U.S. government does have some influence on U.S. economics. For instance, officials pass laws that they hope will lead to fair business practices and safer workplaces.

The U.S. government features three branches: executive, legislative, and judicial. Congress represents the legislative branch. Members of the Senate and House of

You may already be aware that pennies, nickels, dimes, and quarters are the standard coins used in the United States. Dollar bills in different amounts make up the nation's paper currency, or paper money. The U.S. Department of the Treasury is responsible for the production of the country's money.

↜ Barack Obama was elected president of the United States in 2008.

Representatives make the nation's laws. The president heads the executive branch. This branch is responsible for carrying out the laws. The Supreme Court controls the judicial branch. This part of the government decides important issues related to the country's laws.

How does the government guarantee that one branch does not grow too powerful? The U.S. government operates on a system of **checks and balances**. Each branch has special powers that help limit the powers of the other branches.

Do U.S. citizens have any voice in how the government works? Absolutely! The United States is a **democracy**. The people elect politicians, including the president, to represent them.

The first U.S. flag was adopted in 1777. Lawmakers continued to modify its design through the centuries. The current flag features 13 red and white stripes and a blue rectangle with 50 white stars.

USA FIRST-CLASS

# CHAPTER THREE

# MEET THE PEOPLE

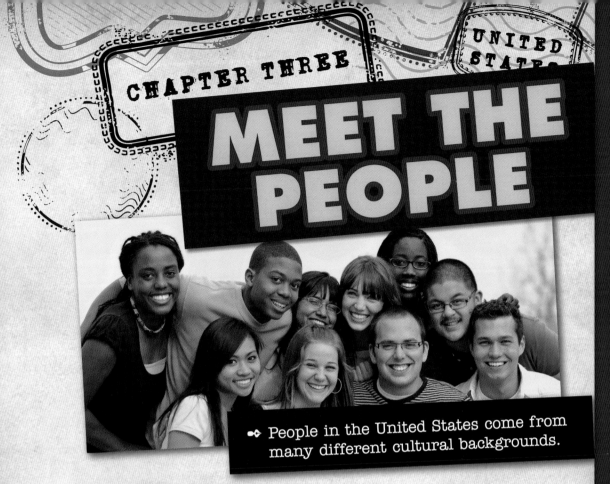

➡ People in the United States come from many different cultural backgrounds.

In 2009, it was estimated that there were more than 307 million people living in the United States. Many of them have ancestors who moved to this country to make a better life. Large numbers of Hispanics became part of the U.S. population when the country took control of territories that belonged to Mexico in the 1800s. Many black Americans are the descendants of people who were brought to the United States as slaves in the early years of the country's history.

Where do all of these people live? Approximately 82 percent of the U.S. population has homes in **urban** areas such as major cities and their suburbs.

21

New York

Los Angeles

What are the United States' most populated cities? In 2008, New York City, New York, claimed 8,363,710 residents. Los Angeles, California, ranked next with 3,833,995 people. Chicago, Illinois, is home to 2,853,114 individuals.

Chicago

Many different cultural groups exist within U.S. borders. Nearly 65 percent of the people are of European Caucasian descent. About 15 percent are Hispanic. Nearly 13 percent are African American. Approximately 4 percent are Asian. American Indians, Alaska Natives, Native Hawai'ians, and Pacific Islanders also make up a part of the population. Many people are of multiracial or multiethnic descent, too.

Native peoples once lived throughout the land that would become the United States. U.S. growth and development, unfortunately, often came at the cost of these native groups. The country's westward expansion during the 1800s is one example. Clashes with American Indians often arose as more settlers headed west. Eventually, the U.S. government forced most tribes to relocate to assigned pieces of land called reservations.

Most people speak English. Through the years, though, many schools and businesses have also presented information in languages such as Spanish. Millions of people in the United States speak other languages, too.

# ACTIVITY

# SPANISH

After English, Spanish is the most popular language spoken in the United States. Do you want to learn some Spanish words and phrases? Look at the lists below. Use a separate sheet of paper and try to match the Spanish words with their English translations. See the answers below.

Spanish
1. escuela (ess-KWAY-lah)
2. hola (OH-la)
3. por favor (POR fah-BOR)
4. casa (KAH-sah)
5. adiós (ah-DYOHSS)
6. gracias (GRAH-see-ahss)

English
a. house
b. thank-you
c. good-bye
d. hello
e. please
f. school

Answers: 1-f; 2-d; 3-e; 4-a; 5-c; 6-b.

➻ Most children and teenagers in the United States attend public schools.

Children and teenagers in the United States are expected to go to school. Most states require citizens between the ages of 5 and 18 to attend classes. Parents can choose to send their children to public schools or private schools. Public schools are free, but private schools charge tuition.

Harvard University was founded in 1636.

After students graduate from high school, they are encouraged to continue their education at a university or technical school. There are more than 4,000 two-year and four-year colleges and universities. Some, such as Harvard University in Cambridge, Massachusetts, are considered to be among the best schools in the world.

Most people value education. Many consider religion to be an important part of their lives, too. People in the United States are free to practice whatever faith they choose.

More than 78 percent of the U.S. population practices some form of Christianity. Approximately 1.7 percent of U.S. residents belong to the Jewish faith. Others follow the principles of Buddhism, Islam, and other faiths.

# CHAPTER FOUR

# CELEBRATIONS

↝ Football is one of the most popular sports in the United States.

The many cultures that exist in the United States have contributed to a variety of pastimes and traditions.

How is a football game a celebration of U.S. culture? A lot of people enjoy gathering to watch live and televised games. Some prefer to play the sport instead. Baseball is popular, too. In addition, many men and women play volleyball or basketball.

U.S. residents like going to the movies or watching television. Many people enjoy concerts and theatrical performances. Museums and zoos attract many visitors, too. Many also take vacations to well-known attractions such as the Grand Canyon in Arizona or Walt Disney World Resort in Florida.

Have you ever heard "The Star-Spangled Banner" sung at the beginning of a baseball game? During World War II (1939–1945), people started the tradition of playing the national anthem before sporting events to celebrate their patriotism.

U.S. residents do not need to travel to another part of the country to have fun, though. They can simply spend time with friends and family during holidays. People often get together on Independence Day. This holiday falls on July 4 every year. Some people host picnics or barbecues on Independence Day. Others watch parades or fireworks displays. Many raise the U.S. flag. People use these activities to remember how early leaders formally adopted the Declaration of Independence on July 4, 1776.

Many cities plan fireworks displays to celebrate the 4th of July.

# CRAFT ACTIVITY

Would you like to create your own U.S. flag? You may want to refer to the flag image in Chapter 2 as a guide as you work.

MATERIALS:
- Construction paper (white and blue)
- Scissors
- Pencil
- Ruler
- Red crayon or marker
- White crayon or chalk
- Glue
- 1 Popsicle stick

INSTRUCTIONS:

1. Take a piece of white construction paper. Do you notice how the paper has 2 longer sides and 2 shorter sides? Grab a shorter side and fold the paper in half. You should now have 2 equal, rectangular halves.

2. Use scissors to cut along the fold to separate the rectangles.

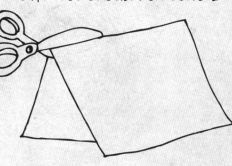

STEP TWO

31

Continued on the following page

3. Lay one rectangle on a flat surface. One of the longer sides of the rectangle should be closest to you. Use a pencil and ruler to outline 13 equally spaced stripes across the length of the rectangle.

4. Color in the stripe at the top of the flag with a red crayon or marker. Leave the next stripe white. The colors of the stripes should continue to alternate from top to bottom. You should have 7 red stripes and 6 white stripes.

5. Use scissors to cut a small rectangle out of the blue construction paper. It should be wide enough to cover the top 7 stripes in the upper left-hand corner of the flag. Again, refer to the Chapter 2 flag image to help guide you.

6. Use your white crayon or chalk to draw 50 stars on the blue rectangle.

7. Glue the blue rectangle onto the upper left-hand corner of your flag.

8. Glue a vertical Popsicle stick behind the left edge of your flag. This is your flagpole.

9. Allow your flag to dry completely.

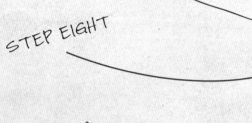

STEP EIGHT

Now wave your flag! Remember, the United States is home to people from many different cultural backgrounds. Try making flags of different countries, too. Maybe you can trace your heritage to another country. Why not make that nation's flag? Or you could simply choose a flag from a country that interests you.

In the United States, people celebrate Thanksgiving on the fourth Thursday of November. Friends and families gather to enjoy a huge feast. Specific dishes may vary, but turkey is usually part of the meal.

The Islamic month of Ramadan is an important time for Muslims. During this time, Muslims do not eat or drink between sunrise and sunset. At the end of Ramadan, Muslims celebrate by getting together and enjoying large meals.

◗ Turkey is part of many Thanksgiving Day dinners.

➽ Muslims often pray at mosques such as this one in Milwaukee, Wisconsin.

Jewish people celebrate holidays such as Yom Kippur. It takes place in September or October. This is a time for Jews to reflect on the year that has passed. They ask for God's forgiveness for any sins they've committed.

Those who practice Christianity often attend Christmas church services and exchange gifts on December 25. From December 26 through January 1, many people participate in Kwanzaa festivities. These celebrations honor family and African heritage and culture.

➥ Some U.S. towns hold parades to celebrate Veterans Day.

Memorial Day is a unique U.S. holiday that takes place on the last Monday of May. It honors members of the U.S. armed forces who have been killed in wars. People in the United States often attend parades or remembrance services on Memorial Day.

November 11 is Veterans Day. This holiday honors those who have served the country in the military. Labor Day falls on the first Monday in September. This day celebrates the efforts of workers.

# CHAPTER FIVE

# WHAT'S FOR DINNER?

◆ Pizza is one popular food in the United States.

Have you ever dined in a Mexican restaurant? Perhaps your favorite is Thai or Chinese food. Eating "American" food means different things to different people.

Remember, the United States is a nation made up of people from many different backgrounds. Many foods that U.S. residents enjoy reflect this. Not all of these dishes originated in the United States, but they are popular with many people who live there.

Do you like pizza? How about spaghetti? Some U.S. families eat these dishes every week. Yet people first began cooking them in Italy. Pizza and spaghetti are examples of how immigrants to the United States have introduced their traditional **cuisines** to this country.

Are there any well-known foods that originated in the United States? Fried chicken, roast turkey, meatloaf, and corn are just a handful of dishes that were first cooked in the United States. So are baked beans and apple pie.

Want to taste a traditional U.S. dessert? Try a cobbler or a buckle. A cobbler is a deep-dish pie with a fruit filling. It is topped with a rich, biscuit crust. A buckle is a kind of cake that is baked in a single layer. It is usually made from a batter containing blueberries.

Certain regions of the country are famous for specific dishes. Are you planning on traveling to the South? Be sure to stop by Louisiana to taste some **Cajun** food. This spicy cuisine combines Southern and French cooking styles. Jambalaya is a famous Cajun dish. It usually contains rice, a protein such as chicken, sausage, or shellfish, and tomatoes, peppers, onions, and celery.

Have you ever been to Texas? The next time you pass through this state, be sure to try chili con carne. This spicy meat-and-bean stew is Texas's official dish. It is also an example of Tex-Mex food, which combines the cuisine of both Texas and Mexico.

chili con carne

❧ New England clam chowder is a creamy, delicious treat!

Maybe you will be visiting the Northeast. Massachusetts is well known for its New England clam chowder. This is a milk-based or cream-based clam stew. If you prefer, you can head to Manhattan, New York, for a different version of the dish. Manhattan clam chowder is also a clam stew. But it contains tomatoes and a clear broth instead of cream or milk.

Many people in the United States look for ways to use fresh, low-fat ingredients when cooking. Smoothies are an example of one popular fresh, low-fat treat. These frozen blended drinks are similar to milkshakes. They are generally considered to be a healthier alternative. That's because they consist of fresh fruit blended with yogurt or milk instead of ice cream.

◆ Smoothies can be made with many different kinds of fruit.

# ACTIVITY

# RECIPE

Want to enjoy a healthy U.S. treat? This smoothie recipe is easy—and tasty! Have an adult help you with the blender and with any slicing.

## Fruit Smoothie

### INGREDIENTS

2 bananas

1 cup strawberries

1 cup blueberries

1 cup (237 milliliters) milk

1 cup (237 ml) plain yogurt

43

Instructions are on the following page

## INSTRUCTIONS

1. Rinse the strawberries under cold water. Pull or carefully cut off their stems.
2. Rinse the blueberries.
3. Peel the bananas.
4. Place all of the ingredients in the pitcher of a blender.
5. Have an adult secure the lid on the pitcher and blend the ingredients for 30 to 60 seconds.
6. Pour the smoothie into 2 glasses.

Enjoy with a family member or friend!

Hot, juicy cheeseburgers are enjoyed by many people in the United States.

Whether you are sipping a smoothie or digging into a pizza, you are getting a taste of U.S. cuisine. These foods and flavors are amazingly diverse—just like the people who enjoy them.

By now, you probably understand that the United States is shaped by a wide variety of beliefs, traditions, and cultures. What part of the country do you want to explore next?

# GLOSSARY

**bayous** (BYE-ooz) swampy, slow-moving streams

**Cajun** (KAY-juhn) having to do with a specific type of spicy cooking

**checks and balances** (CHEKSS AND BAL-uhnss-iz) a system that prevents any one branch of government from becoming too powerful

**cuisines** (kwi-ZEENZ) styles or ways of cooking or presenting food

**deltas** (DEL-tuhz) triangular areas of land that exist where a river divides before entering a larger body of water

**democracy** (di-MOK-ruh-see) a political system in which the people elect leaders to represent them in government

**diverse** (dye-VURSS) made up of varied or different parts or qualities

**endangered** (en-DAYN-jurd) at risk of dying out completely

**exports** (EK-sportss) goods shipped to another country to be sold

**import** (IM-port) to bring a product into a country from another country

**temperate** (TEM-pur-it) having neither very low nor very high temperatures

**urban** (UR-buhn) having to do with cities

# FOR MORE INFORMATION

## Books

Burgan, Michael. *United States of America*. New York: Children's Press, 2008.

Landau, Elaine. *The American Flag*. New York: Children's Press, 2008.

Taylor-Butler, Christine. *The Congress of the United States*. New York: Children's Press, 2008.

## Web Sites

**Central Intelligence Agency—The World Factbook: United States**
*www.cia.gov/library/publications/the-world-factbook/geos/us.html*
Look here for information about the United States' economy, geography, population, and government.

**National Geographic Kids—United States of America**
*kids.nationalgeographic.com/Places/Find/United-states-of-america*
Explore this site for photos and facts about the United States.

**U.S. Census Bureau—State Facts for Students**
*www.census.gov/schools/facts/*
Check out this interactive map and find fast facts about the 50 states plus Puerto Rico.

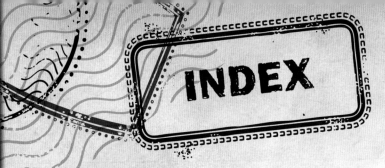

# INDEX

ABOUT THE AUTHOR
Katie Marsico has written more than 60 books for young readers. Her favorite part of the United States is the Gulf Coast of Florida. She would like to dedicate this book to her favorite group of U.S. citizens—Maria, C. J., Thomas, Sara, Emma, Frankie, Matthew, and Nicholas.